# Growing
# Happy
# Kids

By Evelyn Petersen
Illustrated by Barb Tourtillotte

**Totline® Publications**
A Division of Frank Schaffer Publications, Inc.
Torrance, California

*Dedicated with love to my children—Heather, Eric, Karin, and Kristin—and
to their children and grandchildren. I hope that you and other readers of this book
will always make it a priority to take time to enjoy activities with your children.
It is through these experiences that we cherish and honor our childhood memories.
It is during these moments that we pass on both our old and new family traditions.
Keep making moments that will last for lifetimes.     —E.P.*

**Managing Editor:** Kathleen Cubley
**Editor:** Carol Gnojewski
**Contributing Editors:** Gayle Bittinger, Susan Hodges,
   Elizabeth McKinnon, Jean Warren
**Copyeditor:** Kris Fulsaas
**Proofreader:** Miriam Bulmer
**Editorial Assistant:** Durby Peterson
**Graphic Designer (Interior):** Sarah Ness
**Layout Artist:** Gordon Frazier
**Graphic Designer (Cover):** Brenda Mann Harrison
**Production Manager:** Melody Olney

ISBN: 1-57029-101-2

Library of Congress Catalog Card Number 96-61889
Printed in the United States of America
Published by Totline® Publications
**Editorial Office:**   P.O. Box 2250
                Everett, WA 98203
**Business Office:**   23740 Hawthorne Blvd.
                Torrance, CA 90505

20  19  18  17  16  15  14  13  12  11  10  9  8  7  6  5  4  3  2  1

# Introduction

Happy children have positive attitudes about themselves and others that impact the way they cope with stress, changes, relationships, and other challenges they will encounter as they grow to adulthood. In order for children to develop positive attitudes about themselves, they need a strong self-image, which depends upon feeling both lovable and capable.

Feeling lovable has to do with traits that are unique to your child's personality, such as a sense of humor, creativity, friendliness, or perseverance. Children feel lovable when they know that they are appreciated for who they are and not for what they have achieved.

Feeling capable has to do with behaviors that are more like skills, such as being able to listen and follow directions; feeling good about washing, dressing, and getting ready for bed independently; having a sense of who you are and what your limitations might be; and knowing how to be safe and healthy. Children feel capable when they are given the freedom and encouragement to develop at their own pace, make mistakes, and achieve the goals they set for themselves.

Your child's self-image and well-being must be positively reinforced every day. As you read *Growing Happy Kids*, reflect on the ways that you communicate with and respond to your child on a daily basis.

The more aware you become of how your actions and examples affect your child's emotional life, the easier it will be for you to provide him or her with an environment that is truly capable of nurturing a happy, well-adjusted child.

**A WORD ABOUT SAFETY:** The activities in *Growing Happy Kids* are appropriate for young children between the ages of 3 and 5. However, keep in mind that if a project calls for using small objects, an adult should supervise at all times to make sure that children do not put the objects in their mouth. It is recommended that you use art materials that are specifically labeled as safe for children unless the materials are to be used only by an adult.

# Contents

# Feeling
# Loved

# Touch

Nothing beats the power of touch for dispelling fears, frustration, and sadness. Showing your child that he is a huggable, kissable, lovable person will go a long way in helping him gain a positive outlook on life and build self-esteem. Cuddling, hair ruffling, and holding hands are just a few great ways to *communicate* your love.

Try to touch your child lovingly each day. Make it easier for him to communicate his need for affection by keeping a "hug jar" filled with heart-shaped notes. When he gives you a heart, it means he needs a hug.

*A spontaneous, unexpected hug or kiss means a lot.*

# Surprise Gifts

Once in a while, give a simple, tiny gift to your child as a surprise, even if it's not her birthday or a holiday. Wrap it and tag it with her name. The surprise can be a candy kiss, a special fruit, a small book, some crayons, a flower bouquet, or even a pretty shell or stone. It's the message that counts, not the size or value of the surprise.

*Presents are as much fun to open as to receive what's inside.*

# Messages

Caring messages that show up in surprising places and times will make your child feel special.

*The heart shape can show up in many ways that say "I love you."*

- With sidewalk chalk, draw a heart with his name in it in front of your home.

- Put heart stickers on notepaper, and safety-pin the paper to his pillow or slip it under his cereal bowl.

- Send your child a letter or a postcard just for fun. Help him discover the letter in the mail, and then read it to him.

- Make a cardboard frame for a picture of your child. Decorate it with heart-shaped candy and display it on a family bulletin board.

# Special Days

Everyone needs special days to look forward to throughout the year. Designating one day every month as your child's special day is a great way to break out of the routine and show your love. The special day should bring special privileges that you and your child agree on and plan for ahead of time, such as choosing a family game to play, having a friend over, taking a short trip, eating a picnic lunch, planning the day's menu, dressing up, staying up an extra hour, watching favorite videos, or making dessert.

**Birthdays and holidays can seem far apart to a young child.**

# Secret Signals

Children respond to body language much more readily than words. Develop a secret signal to use with your child that means "I love you." This might be a tug on one ear, a thumbs-up signal, a wink, a blink, a hand squeeze, or the gesture for "I love you" in sign language. (Extend your thumb, index finger, and pinkie while bending down your two middle fingers.) Send your love via your secret signal whenever the opportunity arises, and encourage your child to use the secret signal, too. The following are great times to use your secret signal.

*Signing "I love you" is a fun and simple way to show your child you care.*

- In a doctor's or a dentist's office
- At the airport
- On bus or car rides that seem too long
- While talking to someone on the phone
- When your child "takes a back seat" to visitors
- When you're both tired but have errands to run
- To say goodbye at school

# Moments

Moments spent fostering your relationship with your child are subtle but essential ways of saying "I love you." It may sometimes be difficult to find time to relax and enjoy her company, but it is very important. To get started, take note of all the things you've noticed or appreciated about your child throughout the day and share these loving thoughts with her each night before bedtime.

As your child grows older, she will probably forget how organized you were and how clean the house was, but she will always remember the special moments you spent together . . . moments that told her you loved her. Take a few moments to do the following activities with your child.

*Time is a four-letter word that means "I love you."*

- ▨ Make cookies.
- ▨ Find the first star of the evening.
- ▨ Lie on the ground to watch the clouds.
- ▨ Enjoy a moonlight sled ride.
- ▨ Share a nightly bedtime story.
- ▨ Read the Sunday comics in bed.
- ▨ Fly a kite.

# Notice and Share

***Teach your child every day that he is special.***

When you notice traits and behaviors that are special and unique to your child, share them with him, taking the time to be specific. Compliments such as the following help to reinforce the message that your child's specialness has a positive effect on the people around him.

* "No one else has the same special twinkle that you have in your eyes."

* "I don't know anyone else who notices how the plants and flowers in our yard change every day. You are a really good observer."

* "No one giggles the way that you do. Your laugh is contagious. Just hearing you laugh makes me laugh, too."

* "When you listen, you look right into the eyes of the person who is talking. You are a really good listener, and that is a very special gift."

# Tapes

Your child will change and grow quickly, but technology has made it easier to preserve many precious moments in your child's life. Show your child that you value her by tape-recording her voice. Capture her candidly while conversing or telling a story, or have a recording session for her to recite her favorite nursery rhymes and sing her favorite songs. Date the tape and add to it at least once a year.

If you have access to a video camera, videotape your child regularly. Capturing holidays and special events is exciting, but don't stop there. Film your child's everyday activities such as telling you about her paintings or drawings. Film her as she feeds a pet, helps sort the laundry, plays dress up, makes cookies, or plays with family and friends.

*Preserve your child's precious moments for years to come.*

# Being Healthy

# Make it Easy to Be Clean

Children have a natural interest in their body and what they can do with it. Every day, do at least one small thing that shows your child that his body is important. Help him learn how to keep his body clean, fit, and protected from both disease and the elements. Teach him to "tune in" and be aware of the care that his body needs. The following are suggestions for making it easy for your child to stay clean.

*Child-inspired products such as animal-shaped bath mitts, bright-colored hairbrushes, and soap crayons keep grooming activities fun.*

- Put a step stool near the sink, and keep small towels within reach.

- Let him have his own set of towels in his favorite color or personalized with his initials.

- Use liquid soap dispensers, which are easier to handle than slippery bars of soap.

- Use shampoo that does not burn the eyes.

- Let him use baby oil or lotion on his skin to make it soft and sweet-smelling.

- Make sure he washes his hands with soap after toileting and before every snack or meal.

# erms

Use a spray bottle to show your child how germs travel in the air just like a fine spray of water. Tell her that germs are too small to see, and that many germs could fit inside one drop of water. Let her know that germs make people sick, and that we use soap and medicines to kill them and prevent them from spreading. Coughing, sneezing, and touching things with dirty hands are all ways that people spread germs to others. Consider the following disease prevention tips.

*Periodically, clean your child's toys with a bleach and water solution and opt for washable dolls and stuffed animals.*

- Show your child the proper way to sneeze or cough into a tissue, and encourage the habit of throwing it in the garbage can right away.

- If no tissue is available, teach your child how to lift an arm and sneeze or cough into her shoulder.

- Discourage the habit of sharing drinking glasses and plates while eating.

- Have her try to keep fingers clean and away from her eyes, nose, and mouth.

# Immmunizations

Keep a record of all of your child's major illnesses and all shots or immunizations. Get a current copy of recommended immunizations from your pediatrician or children's hospital. Skipping needed immunizations can put your child in danger, so make sure that your child has received each one that is needed. Remember that special boosters and a checkup are needed before entry to kindergarten.

*A family history of disease and illness can be an important diagnostic tool.*

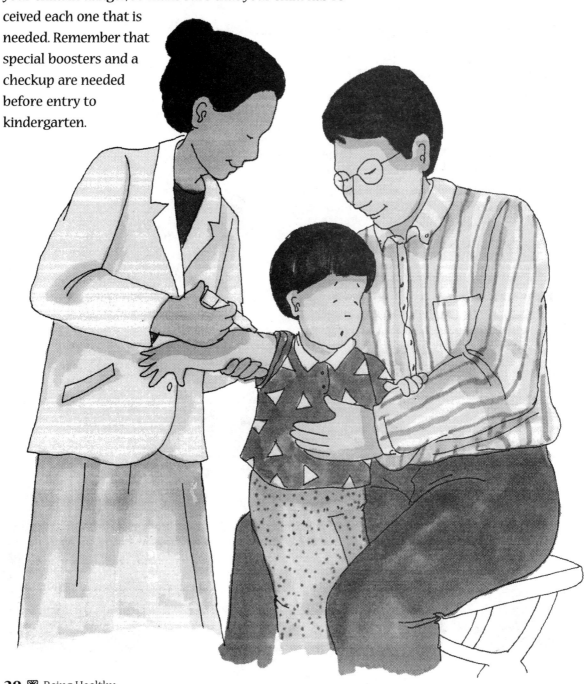

# Fear of Doctors

Prepare your child before a checkup by reading books about going to the doctor or explaining what a doctor does and why it is important for her to be seen by one. With your doctor's permission, take your child to the office just to familiarize her with the building and play with the toys in the reception room. Let her meet the doctor as a friend without the stress of an examination. Reassure her that as a friend, the doctor wants to help her stay well.

Another way to prepare your child for a visit to the doctor is to role-play many of the things that will happen. Have fun and be positive as you pretend the following.

*Knowing what to expect during a visit will ease your child's anxiety about seeing her doctor.*

- Weigh her and measure her height.
- Use a mini-flashlight and tongue depressor to look at her throat and ears.
- Feel her neck as if checking for lumps.
- Tap her kneecap to test her reflexes.
- Listen to her heart and lungs with a toy stethoscope.

Thank your child for her cooperation.

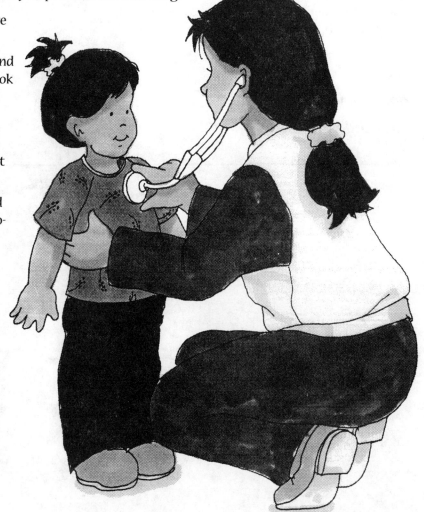

# Fresh Air

Show your child that you value fresh air by spending time outside with him to enjoy the weather. Even if the weather is bad, it's a good idea to play outdoors with your child for at least a few minutes each day. Take a walk, sit on the porch and talk, have a snack in your yard, toss and catch a ball, or play running games.

When you take a fresh-air break, talk about the kinds of clothes, hats, and shoes we wear to protect our bodies when we are outside in different kinds of weather. Bundle yourself up and wear a hat when it is cold, and your child will want to bundle up, too. Wear sunglasses and sun block to take care of your eyes and skin during the spring and summer months, and your child will want to imitate these positive health habits.

***Fresh air breaks are good for you and your child.***

# Eating Right

Plant the seeds for healthy lifetime eating habits by providing your child with healthy foods for mealtimes and snacktimes. Give her fun experiences with healthy foods by letting her scrub or cut up fruits and vegetables to keep handy for snacks. Show her how to prepare simple dips with salad dressing mix and plain yogurt or cottage cheese. Let her dip fresh vegetables in peanut butter or melted cheese. Purchase sugarless cereals and whole grain crackers and breads. Make simple desserts from fresh fruits.

Serve balanced meals at regular times, and make them a pleasant, unhurried family time. Encourage your child to try new foods and to chew slowly and completely before swallowing. Make sure that she drinks plenty of water each day. A special plastic glass or funny ice cube molds will increase her interest in drinking water.

*Set a good example for your child through your own healthy eating habits.*

# Tooth or Consequences

Keeping your child's baby teeth healthy will ensure strong, healthy permanent teeth. Your child will brush best when you are there with him, modeling. Give him his own small tube of toothpaste and a soft-bristled toothbrush, and encourage the habit of brushing teeth after meals and before bedtime. Show him the right way to use his toothbrush to gently reach all of his teeth and scrub them in a circular motion. By the time children are 3, they can also begin to floss their teeth with minimal help.

Sweets and sugared cereals are obvious cavity makers. But also keep in mind that even fruit juices and milk contain sugars that can damage teeth. One of the major causes of tooth decay in young children is letting a toddler carry a bottle filled with juice or milk and suck on it at will. If possible, try to wean your child from a bottle before his first birthday. If your child sleeps with a bottle, or uses it as a security object, keeping it filled with water will not damage his teeth.

*Most dental problems can be prevented by teaching your child good dental health habits.*

# Exercise Breaks

Exercise releases endorphins in the body that keep your child mentally and emotionally upbeat and alert. The natural play activity of preschoolers will lessen as they get older, so establishing a regular exercise habit, even for 10 or 15 minutes a day, is vitally important. A lifetime habit of daily exercise will help your child maintain flexibility, strengthen bones, increase immunity to infection, combat weight problems, and encourage self-esteem. There are so many wonderful benefits of taking just 15 minutes each day for an exercise break. Do it to music and have fun together.

*Help your child experience many different forms of exercise.*

# Stress Busters

Incorporate humor into daily life with funny stories, books, and planned surprises. Humor will help you and your child stay in balance, and keep life's adversities in perspective. Encourage your child's sense of humor by noticing and responding to his jokes and funniness. Surprise your child with your sense of fun whenever possible. If he is pouty or angry, get out a pot, put it on your head, and sit on the counter. Use his laughter to break the tension, and then talk about what's bothering him in a calm, clear way that respects his feelings. But be careful that you don't belittle him or his feelings. Try to risk being funny or spontaneous even if spontaneity doesn't come naturally to you, and encourage your child to risk being silly himself.

Music is another great way for everyone in your family to reduce stress, recharge, and maintain a healthy emotional balance. Use music in your home to create moods of joy, vitality, peace, or relaxation. Share music with your child while you work around the house, exercise, or prepare for naps or bedtimes. Children who enjoy making and listening to music find that it helps them release their aggressive or negative feelings and stay positive. Using pots, pans, and other household items, make simple instruments for your child such as shakers, drums, and cymbals. Or purchase them inexpensively from toy stores. If your child demonstrates a true interest in music or dance, encouraging this talent will have lifelong benefits.

*Music and laughter can positively transform your child's life.*

# Journals

Many people find that the best way for them to maintain balance and emotional fitness is to write out their feelings and thoughts in a daily personal journal. This is such an important avenue for keeping emotionally fit that parents should encourage its beginnings during the preschool years. Your child cannot yet write words about her thoughts and feelings, but you can. Provide her with blank books or scrapbooks and encourage her to tell you a little about her day or her feelings about it. Try to write in the journal almost every day.

Keep it simple. Do not expect more than a sentence. Give your child the option of making a drawing to express herself instead of using words, or of illustrating what you have written for her. Always remember that you are encouraging a wellness habit and not a diary or an original manuscript.

***Focusing on emotional fitness is just as important as keeping physically fit.***

# Being
# Positive
# About Me

# Photos

No one else looks just like your child, and a photograph of your child alone, with the rest of the family, or with friends will make your child feel proud and loved. Creatively displaying photographs of your child throughout your home is a great way to show her how unique she is, and make her feel special at the same time. Here are just a few ideas to try.

- Have a favorite candid photo of your child enlarged to poster size and hang it in her room or your family room.

- Get a special frame that holds several pictures at once, and add a new photo of your child each year to show how she has changed. Or use one picture frame and put the new photo over the old one each year.

- Take "funny face" pictures together in an arcade booth and use them to decorate your refrigerator.

- Tape your child's photo to the center of a play dollar bill (such as the play dollars used in the board game Monopoly) and make multiple copies of the play money for use in pretend play and sorting games.

FUNNY MONEY NOTE
$ Legal tender
4 years old
$ ONE PRESCHOOLER $

***A picture is worth a thousand words!***

# All About Me Book

One of the best ways for your child to feel valued and unique is to keep a book of his early life experiences that he can refer to and add onto with your help. Your child will feel proud and special when he is able to "read" and talk about this written evidence of himself and his personal history. Include a picture of your family, your house, and your neighborhood. Encourage your child to make drawings of his room, his pets, and his friends, and to select a few paintings and art projects to keep inside the book or decorate the covers. Let him tell you about his favorite toys, foods, colors, and videos, as well as his current fears or dislikes. Add to the "Me" book regularly.

*Your child will read his "Me" book often and proudly.*

# Your Child's Name

Whether you picked your child's name out of a name book or chose to honor a favorite friend or relative, your child will enjoy knowing the history of her name. Make her name special to her by celebrating it in the following ways.

*Your child's name is a symbol of herself and her uniqueness.*

- Put her name and date on every art project.

- Add her name to food by dripping pancake batter to form her initials, using candy sprinkles to put her name on cupcakes, or writing her name with catsup or mustard on sandwiches.

- Name some of her favorite foods or cookies after her.

- Have her put her name and a drawing on a sheet of construction paper and let her use it as a placemat. Cover it with self-stick paper to make it reusable.

- Keep a personalized folder for her drawings, dictated stories, and creations.

- Buy her personalized notepads and pencils.

# Mirrors

It's as important to your child's self-esteem to learn to say something good about herself every day as it is to learn to accept the compliments of others. Make it easy for your child to admire her reflection by giving her a child-safe hand mirror, hanging a full-length mirror in her bedroom, or making sure that some of the mirrors in your home are hung at her eye level. Provide a stepladder or a stool so that she can climb up and look at herself in your mirror with you. Point out how many teeth she has, what color her eyes are, and how grown-up she looks in her new clothes. Help her appreciate and express pleasure in her own appearance by asking questions such as the following.

*Self-acceptance is all-important for children of all ages.*

- "Do you like your little smile? Your great big smile?"
- "Can you see your dimple?"
- "Do you like what you chose to wear today?"
- "What do you see that you like about yourself?"

# Outgrowing

Save just a few of your child's outfits, shirts, or shoes as they are outgrown. Be sure to save his baby shoes! When you do your annual closet and drawer cleaning, involve your child. Show him the clothes or the shoes he has outgrown, and have him compare them to his current ones. Your child will take pleasure in this visual evidence of his physical growth.

*Teach your child about sharing the clothes he has outgrown.*

# Coloring

Make your child aware that her coloring is unique to her, and that this uniqueness can be a source of personal pride. Discover and compare the similarities and differences in the coloring of the skin tones and facial features of each member of your family. Does your child have dark brown eyes like Dad? High cheekbones like Mom? Freckles like her sister? Or does she have physical traits that resemble other family members she cares about?

Look through magazines with your child and find pictures of people who have hair that is similar to her hair in color, texture, or style, or eyes of similar shape and color. Follow up on this activity by pointing out the beauty and variety of colors in other living things such as birds, fish, and animals.

*Physical differences are interesting and make us special.*

# Athletic Ability

**Daily exercise makes children aware of what their bodies can do.**

Exercise with your child each morning or evening in front of a mirror, if possible. Play a "Do What I Do" game by taking turns leading stretches. The bending and stretching that you do together will not only increase your child's flexibility, but his awareness of his physical self as well. Stretching in front of a mirror will make him aware of how he looks when he moves, and may help him develop graceful movements or better posture.

# Body Pictures

Purchase a large roll of white butcher paper and secure a 5-foot length of it to the floor with tape. Have your child lie down lengthwise on the paper. Using a thick marker, draw the outline of her whole body. Be sure to add a few distinctive details such as her hat, tennis shoes, suspenders, or a favorite patterned shirt. Then let her draw or paint on her body picture. When your child is finished, cut out her body picture and write her name and the date on the top of one shoe. Hang the picture in a place of honor in your home, such as the kitchen, the family room, or your child's bedroom.

*Make new body pictures regularly and compare the changes.*

# Personal Space

Give your child some personal space by identifying places in your home that are special safe places for him to play, read, store personal treasures, and be alone. This not only helps foster responsibility, but it also helps him develop a willingness to cooperate in shared family spaces. Your child will be proud to see his space in your home identified with his name and his self-portrait or photo. Personalize his bedroom door, his part of a closet, his toy chest, his desk, and his favorite chair, as well as his books, his clothes, his toothbrush, and his special toys. Give him art supplies of his very own, and keep them in a shoebox with his photo on the lid. Help your child label it with his name and the words "Art Box."

*Everyone needs privacy, and your child is no exception.*

# Sexuality

A very important part of your child's attitudes about herself include her sexual identity. Children begin to learn positive sexual attitudes from the moment they are born, through feeding, skin-to-skin touching, cuddling, bathing, and massaging. Perpetuate these positive sexual attitudes by being natural and calm about her interest in her body, or in your body when you are in the bathroom, dressing, undressing, or wearing fewer clothes in hot weather. Try to react positively and objectively when she wants to look at other children's bodies to see how they differ.

To enable your child to grow up with a healthy attitude about her body and the sexual feelings which are a basic and a natural part of life, you need to be willing to answer honestly all of her questions about her body or sex. Let her know that you want her to feel good about her sexuality and gender, and that you are open to any questions she may want to ask.

Consult your local bookstore or library for more information about sexuality and how to teach it positively to your child.

*The question is not whether, but how well, you will teach your child about her sexuality.*

# Being Friendly

# What Is a Friend?

When you talk to your child about friendships, let him know that a friendship is a responsibility. Friends make each other feel good. They talk and listen to each other; take turns; share toys, ideas, interests, and feelings; and laugh and have fun together. Friends don't say mean things about each other and they care about what happens to each other. Friends can be of all ages and sizes. They may look different from you and from each other, but that's OK. Friends will have other friends besides you, and you can have as many or as few friends as you want.

***Friends are beautiful flowers in the garden of life.***

# Making Friends

Making friends is a learned social skill; children are not born with it. Although some children make friends more easily than others, this is a skill that any child can learn or improve upon. You can help your child learn how to make and keep friends by encouraging her to practice the following strategies.

*Teaching your child to make friends is important in a world where people change jobs and locations frequently.*

- Smile and greet others by name.
- Share and take turns.
- Be interested in what others are doing and ask them questions.
- Listen carefully and look into the eyes of others when they speak.
- Give compliments that you really mean.
- Stick up for those who are already your friends and say good things about them.

# Making New Connections

**Look for ways to help your child form new connections whenever your family moves.**

If your family is uprooted and has to move away, your child will need to learn how to make new connections with others. Even if you keep in close touch with old friends, making new connections and participating in new groups is never a wasted effort. These are life skills that you can teach your child through your modeling and encouragement.

Join religious or community groups and involve your child in their activities. Take your child with you to help out when you volunteer for neighborhood or community events. Help him make friends through a child care center, your neighborhood, or a play group you start yourself. Encourage his interest in activities that will help him meet new friends and feel connected to various groups.

# Expressing Yourself

In order to make and keep friends, your child will need the confidence and ability to communicate her needs to other people. Some children are naturally outspoken, but if your child is shy about speaking around other people, she may need help practicing this skill.

Help your child become aware of her body language and facial expressions as she speaks. Demonstrate how much easier it is to talk to someone and ask questions if you look that person in the eye instead of looking at the floor.

Try not to assume or guess in advance what your child wants. Instead, ask her to tell you. When you're with her, don't speak for her, but ask her if she would like to do the telling. Make it clear that it's all right to speak up politely to tell others if she needs something at home, at school, or anywhere else.

*Self-confidence stems from the security of feeling lovable and capable.*

# Playing With Friends

When your child plays with friends, encourage games that foster cooperation rather than competition. Also, plan activities in which everyone participates and is a "winner." Below are a few suggestions.

*Help your child plan cooperative games and activities to enjoy when friends come to play.*

- ▩ Take a nature walk and collect moss, stones, seed pods, and twigs to glue onto individual pieces of wood or cardboard.

- ▩ Together, hold on to the edges of an old sheet and wave it up and down while the children take turns running under it.

- ▩ Act out a favorite story such as "The Three Little Pigs" or "Goldilocks and the Three Bears."

- ▩ Make a snack together and eat it.

- ▩ Make modeling dough together and play with it.

- ▩ Make and decorate cookies to give to a neighbor.

- ▩ Attach pictures to craft sticks to make puppets, and have a puppet show.

- ▩ Use crayons or markers to make a mural on a roll of paper or several large sheets of paper taped together.

# Welcome!

Whenever relatives or friends are coming to visit, work together as a family to make a welcome sign or a banner. For the sign, find a large piece of posterboard or paper. For the banner, tape sheets of paper together or use an extra-long piece of continuous computer paper. Using brightly colored paint or markers, write on the sign or banner some words of welcome and the names of those who will be arriving. Then let your child help add decorations such as smiley faces or scribbled designs.

*Show your child the fun of helping to make others feel welcome in your home.*

# How to Teach Sharing

**With persistence and patience, you can teach your child to share.**

Young children need to learn that some things are their own (a blanket or special stuffed animal) and do not have to be shared unless they are willing. Other toys or materials are things we share with brothers, sisters, and/or visiting friends. A few of these are outside play equipment, the sandbox, blocks, books, and homemade modeling dough.

Help your child take turns by saying, "You've had a long turn to play with that. Let your brother have a turn now, and later you can have another turn." Or, "We have lots of crayons and paper. You can use the blue crayon while she uses the red one, and then you can trade." Or, "He doesn't have any modeling dough. You have a really big pile; can you please give him some of yours so that everyone can play?" Or, "You can take turns with the bucket and shovel, and while you wait for your turn you can use this can and big spoon. Then you can trade."

When children know they have not lost total ownership of a toy or a material and that there is time for everyone to have a turn, they become more comfortable with the idea of sharing.

# Stages of Play

Children do not learn overnight or at a certain age to have friends and play cooperatively. They go through stages as described below. Think of these stages as milestones in your child's social development.

- *Solitary Play*
  (Infant to Toddler)
  Your child plays alone with her toys, fingers, and feet. She observes other children playing, but does not interact.

- *Parallel Play*
  (Toddler to 3 years)
  Your child plays next to another child, or even with the same pile of blocks, but does not interact with the child.

- *Cooperative Play*
  ($3\frac{1}{2}$ to 5 years)
  Your child starts to interact with others in small groups as they use toys and materials. She begins to learn how to share and take turns. Gradually, she learns to play with others and to start building skills in communicating, negotiating, and compromising.

Some children move through these stages faster than others, but don't worry about speed. Instead, help your child by encouraging positive interactions at whatever stage she has reached.

**Recognize and celebrate your child's stages of play.**

# Feeling Capable

# Following Directions

When your child enters school, he will need to listen to and remember directions with several parts ("Close your book, stand up, and come to the door") and do them in order. To practice this skill at home, play directions games with your child. Make up silly, sequential directions such as "Take off one shoe, put it on your head, and then clap your hands." Let your child give you silly directions, too. He will continue to practice this memory skill as he watches you follow his directions.

*Whenever you ask your child to do something, you teach him to follow directions.*

# Basic Information

Reassure your child that if she is separated from you, lost, or in need of help, being able to give basic information about herself to an adult will help solve the problem.

*Teach your child basic information about herself and where she lives.*

Fear or stress may make your child forget, so pretend it is a memory game, and practice with her until she's learned the information by rote and it's as easy for her to do as breathing. Have her recite this information to other adults such as friends, teachers, and relatives, both in person when you aren't in the room and over the telephone. Discreetly label the inside of your child's tote, lunchbox, and coat with this information and make her aware of what these labels mean. It's important that your child can relate the following information.

- Her full name
- Her parents' names
- Her home address and phone number (including area code)
- The full name of a trusted friend, neighbor, or guardian
- The name of her school or day care

# Safe in Public

**Teach your child simple safety techniques.**

When you visit public places such as parks, shopping centers, libraries, and grocery stores with your child, make his safety a priority. Set clear rules about staying close, looking but not touching, and being polite to, but wary of, strangers. Consider these public safety tips.

* Try to avoid shopping or attending events when your child is tired, hungry, or ill. He will not be able to think clearly about his safety.

* Help your child identify people who can help him if he gets lost. Familiarize him with places such as cash registers, information booths, and service desks where store employees are likely to be found. Point out uniforms, name tags, badges, and special hats that set service employees apart from the general public.

* Teach your child to stay where he is if he gets lost. He is never to walk toward exits or wander out into the parking lot if he can't find you.

* Set up a safety drill in your home in which you and your child make believe that you have been separated at a store. Pretend that you are a store employee, and have your child practice asking you for help.

# Neighbors

Get to know your neighbors and introduce your child to the ones you trust. Find out who is likely to be home during the day and night, and who would be willing to watch your home or your child in case of an emergency. Then take a tour of your neighborhood with your child and point out neighborhood landmarks such as friendly neighbors' homes, stores, construction sites, parks, phone booths, and mailboxes. As you walk, help her recognize traffic safety signs and understand what they mean. Teach her to watch for cars on the road, in driveways, and in alleys. Discuss which areas of the neighborhood are safe or unsafe for play. Make her aware that creating safe neighborhoods is a team effort by joining or organizing a neighborhood watch program.

*Make your child aware of the potential dangers in her surroundings.*

# Fire Safety

Talk about and role-play fire safety with your child. Focus on fire safety practice as a game of pretend, but make it clear that the skills you are teaching him will keep him safe in case of a real fire emergency. Your practice drills should include tips for preventing smoke inhalation such as keeping low to the ground where the air is easier to breathe, as well as the following.

- Practice dialing 911 with the phone unplugged.

- Practice using the "stop, drop, and roll" technique in case his clothes catch on fire.

- Locate the fire extinguisher in your home and demonstrate how it is used.

- Locate your smoke alarms and let him hear what they sound like.

- Develop several fire escape plans.

- Take a tour of your local fire station and ask for free safety posters, pamphlets, stickers, and activity coloring books.

- Emphasize the importance of getting out of the house rather than hiding from a fire.

*Make sure that your child has a healthy respect for the destructive potential of matches, lighters, and open flames.*

# Gun Safety

Handguns and firearms in the home pose a grave danger to children. If you own a firearm, it is your responsibility to put a gun lock on the trigger, and keep the gun safely locked away. Consider carrying the key to your gun cabinet or case on a keychain, belt, or necklace. If you are wearing or carrying the key, you will know where it is at all times, and this will prevent your child from gaining access to it. For extra insurance against accidents, teach your child about firearm safety. Educate her about guns not to instill fear, but to increase a realistic understanding of their dangers.

*Knowing what to do around a gun is a safety skill that may save your child's life.*

Here are four basic rules that your child should follow if she finds or sees a gun.

- Stop.
- Don't touch.
- Leave the area.
- Tell an adult.

# Safe Inside

**Enable your child to learn and practice ways to be safe on his own.**

Hopefully you will never need to leave your young child unattended. However, in case of an emergency, your child should know how to stay safe in your home. Designate a childproof room or rooms for him to play in if circumstances prevent you from keeping a close eye on him. Teach him the following safety tips, and make sure that your child knows why they are important.

- Stay inside the house at all times.
- Keep all doors and windows locked.
- Never open the door to anyone but immediate family members.
- Never tell anyone that you are alone.
- Call 911 if you are afraid.
- Don't answer the telephone.
- Set up a system of alerting close neighbors when there's an emergency, such as tying a red ribbon on your doorknob or hanging an ornament in a window.
- Be aware of all exits in case of fire.

# Good Listener

Here are a few games that will encourage your child to listen more effectively.

*Notice and listen to sounds both inside and outside.*

- Make a game of closing your eyes, listening carefully, and trying to point in the direction of a specific sound source.

- Make a sound matching game by placing small items such as buttons, paper clips, coins, and dried beans in pairs of empty plastic film containers. Tape the lids securely closed. Have your child shake the containers to find the pairs with the matching sounds.

- Help your child make sounds with objects found around your house such as kitchen utensils, jar lids, bottle caps, tea balls, straws, and crumpled paper.

- Encourage your child to make sounds for you to guess.

- Always model good listening yourself! Your child will learn the most from your modeling.

# Being Emotionally Secure

# Accepting Praise

Some children have difficulty accepting praise because it makes them feel self-conscious. Children who have problems accepting praise graciously may begin to discount the praise they receive and believe they are unworthy of it. Teach your child how to accept a compliment with a response that feels comfortable to him. Explain that if he's not sure he understands or really agrees with someone's praise, he can still say, "Thank you for saying that" or "Thank you, I'm glad you like it."

Encourage him to generate a response, even if he's still shy about it. With time, he'll gain the confidence to respond to praise in a more genuine way.

**Praise helps children only if they have learned to react to it positively.**

# Establishing Routines

Establishing some continuity in your family life is important to your child's well-being. If your child attends a day-care center or a preschool, find out how naps, snacktime, and outside play times are scheduled so that you can coordinate this schedule with your weekend and after-care activities. If you can, try to eat meals together at about the same time each day. Try even harder to establish regular bedtime hours and a nightly bedtime routine. Consistent bedtime routine will give your child a sense of security that will help her sleep better. Make bedtime a sharing time by reading together or making a healthy bedtime snack with her on a regular basis.

*It's important to follow regular routines and rituals each day.*

# Security Objects

*Favorite dolls or blankets are important to the emotional stability of your child.*

Many young children find it easier to deal with their feelings if they have the comfort and reassurance of a favorite blanket, doll, or stuffed animal. If your child uses a security object, respect this behavior as a genuine need and a positive step in his emotional growth. Some children need their security objects most of the day; others use them only when they feel vulnerable, such as with new people, in new surroundings, or at bedtime. Let your child keep his security objects until he is ready to give them up. If you give him free rein to indulge this need, he will eventually gain the confidence and independence to outgrow it. Sometimes the responsibility of a pet, such as a guinea pig, a puppy, or a kitten, can help ease this transition.

# Experiencing Fears

Being in control of your fears is a reassuring feeling that boosts confidence and self-esteem. When children can put their fears into words and describe them to others, it helps them regain control.

***Help your child realize that all of her feelings are important.***

If your child is having trouble coping with something that is frightening her, let her draw or paint what is scary to her, and encourage her to talk about her drawing. Can she give her fear a name? A sound? A walk?

Help your child come up with strategies for confronting and dealing with this scary thing. The more familiar your child becomes with her fears, the easier it will be for her to overcome them.

# Puppets and Props

Hand puppets and other props create a safe, make-believe zone that provides just enough distance from reality to enable your child to feel less vulnerable about his strong feelings. Children who are just learning how to express their feelings may also find that it's easier to respond to puppets than to people. With the help of the following tools, it may be easier for your child to open up to you.

*Sometimes special tools are needed to help children share their feelings.*

- ▨ A hand puppet that talks for your child (keep a puppet on hand for yourself, too, so that it can answer your child's puppet and give advice and reassurance)

- ▨ A magic mirror that reflects exactly how he feels inside

- ▨ A magic carpet or carpet square that will take your child wherever he wants to go

- ▨ A magic lamp to tell his wishes to

- ▨ A bottle filled with a magic potion that can change him into whatever he wants to be

- ▨ A magic cape that makes your child invisible, but gives voice to his secret feelings

- ▨ Face puzzles, masks, or dolls whose faces he can manipulate to reflect his mood

# Individual Interests

Your child's interests will grow and change with time. However, it's important to encourage and nurture them as they appear. The individual interests that she develops outside of home, day care, or preschool will help put balance and enjoyment in her life both now and in the years to come, and enable her to form friendships with children with like interests.

Be aware of what your child enjoys. If, for example, she's thrilled by trains, take her on a train ride, read books about trains, and let her help you design a train birthday cake. The support, enthusiasm, and guidance that you provide will give her the courage to risk and explore further avenues of interest.

*Interests and hobbies help children stay emotionally fit.*

# Emotional Safety

Your child needs to feel emotionally safe as well as physically safe. The most important way to foster emotional security is to create an atmosphere of trust and sharing so that your child feels confident about expressing his worries without fear of ridicule or embarrassment. Make your child aware that you are willing to help him if he has a problem, and that many adults such as teachers, close friends, and relatives can help, too. Your child needs to know you'll listen to his problems without interruption and treat his worries and fears as important, legitimate concerns. He also needs to feel you'll understand and try to help when he's let his worries overwhelm him. This kind of respectful communication is an emotional safety net that will make your child feel competent and cherished.

*Teachers, relatives, and close family friends can be relied on for support.*

# Death and Loss

*Young children sometimes fear that they might be left alone or abandoned.*

Children often experience loss and loneliness when parents are away at work or on a trip. But when a special loved one moves far away or dies, your child's loneliness may be mixed with the fear and anxiety that you might go away, too, and not come back. At such times you must be especially aware of your child's need for security. Let her know where you are at all times. Call her if you are apart, and give her extra comfort when you are together. If you are honest about your own feelings of sadness, it will help her know that you understand and share her feelings. Tangible tokens of your love, including your photo and special family symbols, will help your child feel less lonely when you are not together, and focusing on happy memories will help her gradually accept the loss.

# Safety-Proof

Safety-proof your home and include your child in this process so that he's aware of potential safety hazards and the steps you have taken to prevent them.

*Families that live in safe, childproof houses have peace of mind.*

- Store electrical appliances away from sinks, tubs, and toilets.
- Cover unused electrical outlets.
- Place danger stickers on medicines and household cleaning materials.
- Put safety locks on cabinets or place all hazardous substances completely out of reach.
- Keep emergency phone numbers next to each phone, and teach your child how to dial 911.
- Tape long electrical cords securely to the floor.
- Use proper gates or locks to close off stairways.

# Natural Disasters

*Controlling a make-believe storm during pretend play will help your child stay calm during a real one.*

If you live in an area where tornados, hurricanes, or other weather emergencies occur, be sure to practice with your child what to do. Talk about what happens during these storms, and choose a safe place to wait them out, such as a bathroom, closet, cellar, or basement. Being prepared gives your child a plan of action in the event of a storm watch. Let your child help you prepare a natural disaster kit with a working flashlight, batteries, matches, bandages, a can opener, a Swiss army knife, and enough food and water to keep everyone in your family fed for three days.

Create a pretend storm by showing your child how to drum her fingers on a tabletop for rain sounds and by howling and blowing to simulate wind. Shake a large aluminum roasting pan for thunder crashes, and use a flashlight for lightning. Make the storm sounds get louder and louder, and then let them fade away so that your child experiences the storm as it approaches and passes on. If she is afraid of storms, this kind of pretend practice will ease her fears about them, because when she pretends, she can control the storm's intensity.

# Feeling OK About Being Imperfect

# Make a Mess

**Make equal room for messiness and order in your home.**

Every so often, making a big mess with your child will take the pressure off him to always be tidy both inside and outside your home. Try some of the activities below. If you control the where, what, and when of these activities, they'll be a source of shared laughter and good memories.

- Play in mud puddles on a spring day.
- Make mud pies and cookies and "bake" them on the front porch.
- Squirt unscented shaving cream into the bathroom sink and decorate the bathroom mirror.
- Fingerpaint with whipped cream or pudding.
- Make homemade modeling dough on the kitchen table.
- Write on your tub and tiles with soap crayons.

# Be Realistic

Young children need to explore their environment with their whole bodies, so getting dirty is part of their daily work and play. If your child is never allowed to get dirty or make a mess, she may develop the unhealthy and unrealistic attitude that she must always be "perfect." Keep this in mind when you dress your child for everyday play activities. Don't expect her to stay perfectly clean and unrumpled even if she's dressed in her Sunday best for a special event.

Provide your child with clothes that are sturdy, machine washable, and which allow for freedom of movement. Teach her a few simple but consistent rules about where to take off her shoes, where to put her dirty clothes, and when and how to clean herself up. If your child attends a child-care facility or a preschool, or when she visits family or friends, be sure to bring along at least one complete change of clothing, just in case.

*Unreasonable expectations are a heavy burden.*

# Helpful Criticism

*If focused on helping, not hurting, criticism can promote an inner sense of responsibility.*

Constructive criticism is a way to help your child change his behavior or improve at an activity without making him feel bad about himself. Offer positive suggestions for improving his performance, and involve him in finding ways to do things differently. For example, if he's playing in the water instead of actually washing the dishes, you might say, "Sometimes I like to make mounds out of soapsuds too, and you've made some really big ones, but that took a long time. If you use these soapsuds on the dishes and put them here to rinse, we can finish this job quickly. Then we'll have time to play outside."

Invite your child to think of other ways to keep jobs fun while still getting the work done. This kind of problem solving will teach him how to take responsibility for his behavior and become personally involved in improving it.

# Sharing Feelings

Create a sharing time each day to help your child talk about her feelings. Try to choose a quiet time of the day when she is settled and less distracted, perhaps after supper or just before bedtime. Take the lead by sharing some of the emotions that you felt during the day. Then invite your child to talk about her day. Let her know that it's OK for her to have both positive and negative feelings.

*Reassure your child that all of her feelings are valid.*

- "I felt tired and sad when I got home from work because it seemed like such a long day and I missed you."

- "How did you feel when the sun came out today? I felt very happy about it."

- "I was worried when I drove to the store with you because there was ice and snow on the road."

- "I had fun making pizza with you this evening. How did you feel about helping me cook?"

# Risking

Let your child see you try new things, even if you fail or don't do them well. If he sees that you can make mistakes and laugh at yourself, and that you don't need to do something perfectly to enjoy it, he will be able to risk mistakes and be more willing to pick himself up and try again if he isn't immediately successful. Model how to handle mistakes positively by talking about what might have happened and what you will do differently next time. If you try a new recipe and it fails, invite him to help you find out what went wrong. Make plans to try it again together soon.

*Every day we experience things that don't go perfectly.*

# Fear of Failure

*Children who are expected to always be perfect often develop fragile self-esteem.*

Some children, particularly those of successful parents, are reluctant to risk making mistakes. They believe that if you can't be sure you'll do things perfectly, it's better not to try them at all. The mistakes themselves are less damaging than the belief that a mistake can make you a failure. If you have a child who feels this way, you may actually need to teach her to take small risks and make errors so that she will learn that mistakes are not tragic. Your child needs to know that she can fail and still be loved. She needs to accept mistakes as a necessary part of being human and to know that they don't detract from her overall competency. When your child makes a mistake, try emphasizing all of the things she did right.

- "You can tell me if you goofed; I've made lots of mistakes today, too."

- "I know you feel bad about the broken cup, but it's OK. It could happen to anyone."

- "You did lots of things right today. Let's talk about them instead."

# Memories

Making mistakes is a big part of learning and growing. An important step in your development as a parent is to honor the mistakes you've made in the past and to let your children have room to make mistakes of their own. If you're reluctant to admit your mistakes, then your child may be intimidated by his perception that you're perfect. He may then find it difficult to acknowledge his own mistakes or talk to you about them.

Encourage your child to feel more comfortable with mistakes by talking about the mistakes you made when you were his age. Discuss how you felt about them at the time, and how you overcame them and learned from them. Above all, make it clear that your love for him doesn't lessen when he makes mistakes. Let him know he can turn to you when he's troubled or in trouble.

**_Tell stories about how you handled mistakes when you were a child._**

# Parent or Buddy?

Some parents, especially single parents, tend to regard their children as their best friends. While it's great to be your child's friend, it's important to remember that you are also her parent. If you treat your child as an equal or a confidant, you may be putting her in a position for which she is unprepared.

When you have heart-to-heart talks with your child, leave out adult details. Avoid giving her information or responsibility for which she is too young by asking her to help you make adult decisions. Keep in mind that you're still the one who makes final decisions on all the rules.

*You can be your child's friend, but being a parent has to come first.*

# Role-Play

Look around the house for props and dress-up clothes to use for role-playing activities. Act out your child's favorite stories, or make up stories that will enable him to act out different feelings. In your dress-up personas, have pretend confrontations and find solutions to pretend problems. Switch roles midstory or act out a story more than once so that you and your child can take turns being different characters. Below are suggestions for role-playing props.

*Role-playing is a great way to teach your child to empathize with others.*

- Scarves, bandannas, and handkerchiefs
- Hats
- Small totes or suitcases
- Jewelry
- Fabric scraps
- Wigs
- Briefcases
- Calculators
- Fake fur
- Oversize shoes
- Old coats
- Old dresses
- Sunglasses or eyeglass frames with the lenses removed
- Backpacks
- Old or toy cameras

# She's Just Shy

Try not to make assumptions or label your child as shy or outgoing, introverted or extroverted. Generalizing could lead you to expect a certain kind of behavior of her, or to expose her to certain experiences and not to others. It also can give her an incorrect perception of herself. For example, some children who are labeled shy are very strong-willed and persistent individuals. When they watch others on the playground or wait for a rowdy group in line to disperse, they are being observant, not shy.

Some children become drained when they interact with or talk to others. They need personal space to be alone in and time to relax and recharge. Other children get recharged from interacting with others, and don't work well alone. Some children are very careful about what they share with you because sharing is giving up a piece of themselves. Others share everything with anyone, with no misgivings. To nurture positive attitudes in your child, accept her individual qualities without labeling, and help her identify as individual strengths her unique ways of handling situations.

*All of us are shy in some situations and outgoing in others.*

# Being Family-Oriented

# Sharing the Fun

One of the nicest ways to build your child's self-esteem is to share the joys of laughter and togetherness. Laughter is a wonderful healer and stress reliever. Help your child experience the sheer joy of laughter by loosening up a bit and having fun. Make funny faces at each other, sing silly songs, and tell each other goofy, open-ended stories. Play with his favorite toys or have a fun-filled "snowball fight" inside the house with crumpled-up newspaper snowballs!

*One of the best gifts you can give is laughter.*

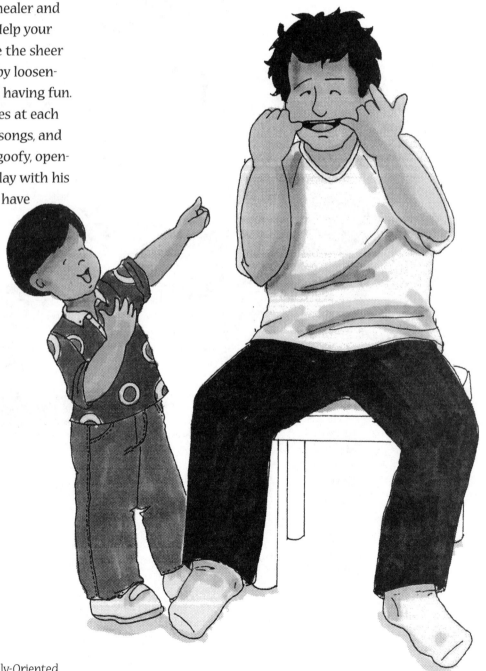

# Little Things Mean a Lot

*Doing everyday things together as a family will mean the most to your child.*

It is not the big, annual vacation that does the most to promote a sense of belonging in the family; it's the ongoing "little things." Below are some small—but important—ways you can help promote feelings of family togetherness for your child.

- Work together on family projects such as making a bird feeder, washing the car, or having a garage sale.
- Make spaghetti together.
- Go on family picnics.
- Schedule family movie nights.
- Work on scrapbooks or photo albums together.

# Active Fun

Doing active, enjoyable things together increases children's feelings of belonging to and cooperating with the family group. Many families engage in such activities as hiking, skiing, fishing, boating, skating, bowling, or cycling, with the children taking part as they become old enough. Include your children in your active family fun as often as possible. Try to arrange a regular day at least once a month to engage in active family fun that your child can participate in safely. For 3-year-olds, you might want to start with simple play such as going for walks, jumping in piles of leaves, or making snow people. Older children can begin to learn the basics of such activities as skating, bike riding, or ball playing.

*When a family plays together and has fun, members are more likely to cooperate.*

# Family Games

*Foster cooperation skills by playing family games in which your child can participate.*

Many families enjoy playing cards or board games together. Try very simple table games with 3- and 4-year-olds such as sorting game pieces by size or color, but don't be afraid to try teaching more challenging games to 4- to 5-year-olds, such as matching cards or dominoes. Play games in which your child can participate and that all ages can enjoy.

For instance, after dinner you could play a progressive-story game in which each person tells just a little of a made-up story and then passes the story on to the next person, who adds to it. Or try the word game called If. To play, ask each person a question such as "If you could be an animal, which one would you be and why?" or "If you could be anyone on TV, who would you be and why?" or "If you could travel anywhere, where would it be and why?" Together, make up your own games to play as a family.

# Gifts and Gift Ideas

**Making gifts for others fosters generosity and teaches your child the joy of giving.**

Make homemade gifts a family tradition, not only at holiday time but any time that gift giving is appropriate. When children make gifts, they learn the good feeling of giving something of themselves to others. Gather and save materials beforehand and arrange some space and time for making the gifts together with your child. You can help him make gifts any time of the year—on summer days when you may have extra time for this kind of family fun, or on rainy days when he needs something to do. Let your child wrap and label the gifts so that they are ready when you need them.

The ideas that follow are easy gifts that you and your child can make together. Try one or more of them. If you wish, let your child make gift-wrap by using thick, colorful tempera paint to stamp handprints on tissue paper or cut-open brown paper bags.

▨ Placemats—Cut shapes from construction paper, gift-wrap, and aluminum foil. Let your child glue the shapes on large pieces of construction paper. Laminate the papers or cover them with clear self-stick paper.

▨ Stationery—Make a stamp by cutting a design in the end of a potato. Let your child dip the stamp in paint and press it on pieces of note paper to make prints.

▨ "I Love You" Book—Have your child tell you what he loves best about a friend or a relative. Write down these thoughts in a blank book and let your child illustrate the pages with crayons or markers.

# Family Scrapbooks

Family scrapbooks can increase your child's sense of belonging in two ways. First, when helping to make the scrapbooks, he will work with other family members to save, sort, arrange, and glue the scrapbook items. Second, he will gain a sense of family togetherness when he looks at completed or in-progress scrapbooks and recalls memories of times past with you.

Designate a few shoeboxes or baskets as holders for saving items such as photos, ticket stubs, postcards from travels, newspaper clippings, school play programs, or wedding and birth announcements. Plan a regular time, at least once a month, to work on the scrapbooks. If you wish, make separate scrapbooks for family camping experiences, family trips, activities with friends, birthdays, holidays, family reunions, and so on. Keep the scrapbooks in a place where you and your child can look at them often.

*Making family scrapbooks is a perfect activity for promoting togetherness.*

# Family Recipe Book

A family recipe book not only nurtures connections within the group, it becomes a tangible symbol of your extended family's uniqueness. Favorite family recipes can be collected and typed, copied, and then inexpensively put into books with spiral bindings.

Before making copies of the book, let your child add dictated comments or line drawings in the margins of your master copy. Or ask him to dictate a recipe for making a favorite dish while you write it down to include it in the book. Be sure to use his exact words. When the book is printed, it will become treasured written evidence of his family connections.

*Your child will take pride in helping to create this family book.*

# Taping Elders' Stories

*Keeping family stories alive is a great way to strengthen togetherness.*

One of the easiest ways to preserve your family history is to tape-record the stories of parents, grandparents, or great-grandparents. Plan a time to do this, and do it casually, without fanfare, when older relatives visit you. Ask them to tell about such things as their funniest experiences, their childhood games, or what they did on weekends when they were little. Tape their stories about going to school, their first job, their most embarrassing moment, or how they met their spouse. Follow up by making a tape that tells about when your child was born or about how you and your child's other parent met. These stories will become invaluable ties to the family for your child. They are part of your family's history and her heritage.

# Title Index

## Activity Books

### BEST OF TOTLINE® SERIES
*Totline Magazine's best ideas.*
Best of Totline
Best of Totline Parent Flyers

### BUSY BEES SERIES
*Seasonal ideas for twos and threes.*
Busy Bees—Fall
Busy Bees—Winter
Busy Bees—Spring
Busy Bees—Summer

### CELEBRATION SERIES
*Early learning through celebrations.*
Small World Celebrations
Special Day Celebrations
Great Big Holiday Celebrations
Celebrating Likes and Differences

### EXPLORING SERIES
*Versatile, hands-on learning.*
Exploring Sand
Exploring Water
Exploring Wood

### FOUR SEASONS
*Active learning through the year.*
Four Seasons—Art
Four Seasons—Math
Four Seasons—Movement
Four Seasons—Science

### GREAT BIG THEMES SERIES
*Giant units designed around a theme.*
Space • Zoo • Circus

### LEARNING & CARING ABOUT
*Teach children about their world.*
Our World
Our Town

### PIGGYBACK® SONGS
*New songs sung to the tunes
of childhood favorites!*
Piggyback Songs
More Piggyback Songs
Piggyback Songs for Infants
  and Toddlers
Holiday Piggyback Songs
Animal Piggyback Songs
Piggyback Songs for School
Piggyback Songs to Sign
Spanish Piggyback Songs
More Piggyback Songs for School

### PLAY & LEARN SERIES
*Learning through familiar objects.*
Play & Learn with Magnets
Play & Learn with Rubber Stamps
Play & Learn with Photos
Play & Learn with Stickers
Play & Learn with
  Paper Shapes & Borders

Totline®
Publications

### 1•2•3 SERIES
*Open-ended learning.*
1•2•3 Art
1•2•3 Games
1•2•3 Colors
1•2•3 Puppets
1•2•3 Reading & Writing
1•2•3 Rhymes, Stories & Songs
1•2•3 Math
1•2•3 Science
1•2•3 Shapes

### THEME-A-SAURUS® SERIES
*Classroom-tested, instant themes.*
Theme-A-Saurus
Theme-A-Saurus II
Toddler Theme-A-Saurus
Alphabet Theme-A-Saurus
Nursery Rhyme Theme-A-Saurus
Storytime Theme-A-Saurus
Multisensory Theme-A-Saurus

## Parent Books

### A YEAR OF FUN SERIES
*Age-specific books for patenting.*
Just for Babies  •Just for Ones
Just for Twos  • Just for Threes
Just for Fours  • Just for Fives

### BEGINNING FUN WITH ART
*Introduce your child to art fun.*
Craft Sticks • Crayons • Felt
Glue • Paint • Paper Shapes
Modeling Dough • Tissue Paper
Scissors • Rubber Stamps
Stickers • Yarn

### BEGINNING FUN WITH SCIENCE
*Spark your child's interest in science.*
Bugs & Butterflies • Plants &
Flowers • Magnets • Rainbows
& Colors • Sand & Shells
• Water & Bubbles

### LEARNING EVERYWHERE
*Discover teaching opportunities
everywhere you go.*
Teaching House • Teaching Trips
Teaching Town

## Story Time
*Delightful stories with related activity
ideas, snacks, and songs.*

### KIDS CELEBRATE SERIES
Kids Celebrate the Alphabet
Kids Celebrate Numbers

### HUFF AND PUFF® SERIES
Huff and Puff's Snowy Day
Huff and Puff
  on Groundhog Day
Huff and Puff's Hat Relay
Huff and Puff's April Showers
Huff and Puff's
  Hawaiian Rainbow
Huff and Puff Go to Camp
Huff and Puff's Fourth of July
Huff and Puff
  Around the World
Huff and Puff Go to School
Huff and Puff on Halloween
Huff and Puff on Thanksgiving
Huff and Puff's Foggy Christmas

### NATURE SERIES
The Bear and the Mountain
Ellie the Evergreen
The Wishing Fish

## Resources

### BEAR HUGS® SERIES
*Encourage positive attitudes.*
Remembering the Rules
Staying in Line
Circle Time
Transition Times
Time Out
Saying Goodbye
Meals and Snacks
Nap Time
Cleanup
Fostering Self-Esteem
Being Afraid
Saving the Earth
Being Responsible
Getting Along
Being Healthy
Welcoming Children
Respecting Others
Accepting Change

### MIX & MATCH PATTERNS
*Simple patterns to save time!*
Animal • Everyday
Holiday • Nature

### PROBLEM SOLVING SAFARI
*Teaching problem solving skills.*
Problem Solving—Art
Problem Solving—Blocks
Problem Solving—Dramatic Play

Problem Solving—Manipulatives
Problem Solving—Outdoors
Problem Solving—Science

### 101 TIPS FOR DIRECTORS
*Valuable tips for busy directors.*
Staff and Parent Self-Esteem
Parent Communication
Health and Safety
Marketing Your Center
Resources for You
  and Your Center
Child Development Training

### 101 TIPS FOR
### PRESCHOOL TEACHERS
Creating Theme
  Environments
Encouraging Creativity
Developing Motor Skills
Developing Language Skills
Teaching Basic Concepts
Spicing Up Learning Centers

### 101 TIPS FOR
### TODDLER TEACHERS
Classroom Management
Discovery Play
Dramatic Play
Large Motor Play
Small Motor Play
Word Play

### 1001 SERIES
*Super reference books.*
1001 Teaching Props
1001 Teaching Tips
1001 Rhymes & Fingerplays

### SNACKS SERIES
*Nutrition combines with learning.*
Super Snacks
Healthy Snacks
Teaching Snacks
Multicultural Snacks

## Puzzles & Posters

### PUZZLES
Kids Celebrate the Alphabet
Kids Celebrate Numbers
African Adventure
Underwater Adventure
Bear Hugs Health Puzzles
Busy Bees

### POSTERS
We Work and Play Together
Bear Hugs Sing-Along
  Health Posters
Busy Bees Area Posters